STAND YOUR GROUND AND LET GOD FIGHT.

STAND YOUR GROUND AND LET GOD FIGHT.

THERESA MOORE

XULON PRESS

Xulon Press
2301 Lucien Way #415
Maitland, FL 32751
407.339.4217
www.xulonpress.com

© 2021 by Theresa Moore

All rights reserved solely by the author. The author guarantees all contents are original and do not infringe upon the legal rights of any other person or work. No part of this book may be reproduced in any form without the permission of the author.

Due to the changing nature of the Internet, if there are any web addresses, links, or URLs included in this manuscript, these may have been altered and may no longer be accessible. The views and opinions shared in this book belong solely to the author and do not necessarily reflect those of the publisher. The publisher therefore disclaims responsibility for the views or opinions expressed within the work.

Unless otherwise indicated, Scripture quotations taken from the King James Version (KJV)–*public domain.*

Scripture quotations taken from The Message (MSG). Copyright © 1993, 1994, 1995, 1996, 2000, 2001, 2002. Used by permission of NavPress Publishing Group. Used by permission. All rights reserved.

Scripture quotations taken from The **Voice** Bible (VB) Copyright © 2012 Thomas Nelson, Inc. The Voice™ translation © 2012 Ecclesia Bible Society All rights reserved.

Scripture quotations taken from the English Standard Version (ESV). Copyright © 2001 by Crossway, a publishing ministry of Good News Publishers. Used by permission. All rights reserved.

Printed in the United States of America

Paperback ISBN-13: 978-1-66284-315-0
Ebook ISBN-13: 978-1-66284-316-7

(preface)

As a people we always like something new. We become captivated, even subjugated, to this or that. A new entertainment series, a new style, a new way of thinking. In our quest for newness, we may find ourselves in old-fashioned bondage to worldly rationalizations. So much has become admissible in the world, but it doesn't make it God's best for us.

There is so much you can subscribe to in our contemporary society. Theories, pundits, sages, politicians, oligarchies, alternative lifestyles, alternative genders, et cetera. The choices are seemingly endless. But yet the unrest and stress in our world is exceedingly high. Worry and fear have captivated our lives. Confusion is more evident than certainty, and absolutes have been exchanged for absurdities. It's time to dismantle our unwavering allegiance to those sources that manipulate our faculties and reasoning and align ourselves to God. Alignment to Jehovah God doesn't diminish our capabilities to have a thinking mind and conscience, it empowers it.

God has given us the power to overcome the enemy and confusion. 1 Timothy 1:7 says, "For God will never give you the spirit of fear, but the Holy Spirit who gives you mighty power, love, and sound mind." In Matthew 18, Jesus says," Whatever we bind on earth will be bound in heaven and whatever we loose on earth will be loosed in heaven."

As God's people we don't need to hear something new, we need to be reminded of what is true. As it says in Luke 10:20, "The great triumph is not your authority over evil, but in God's authority over you and presence with you. Not what you do for God, what God does for you—that is the agenda for rejoicing."

TRUTH: God lives and He doesn't need your permission to do so. TRUTH: We have been created in His image (Genesis 1:27). TRUTH: There will never be any greater cause in our life than God's purpose for us. There will never be a greater relationship than the one you forge with God. Jeremiah 1:5 says, "Before I formed you in the womb, I knew you and before you were born I consecrated you." Nothing can replace this intimate and all-knowing God. Wealth cannot replace him, nor a scientific discovery, government, religion, or any worldly concept or institution. Ten trillion new ideas of identity or purpose will never dwarf our one and only God.

God's intent is clear from Genesis to Revelations. We are to trust in Him alone and be moved by His love in all circumstances.

The incarnation of Jesus gives us a clear picture of what a surrendered life to our Father should be. Jesus was and is Proverbs 3:5 in action. He trusted in the Lord with all His heart and did not lean on His human understanding. In all His ways He submitted to God his Father, so God could make clear His path.

The Holy Spirit is the evidence that God is with us. 1 Corinthians 2:12 states, "What we have received is not the spirit of the world, but the Spirit from God, so that we may understand what God has freely given us. God's Spirit searches out everything and reveals the deep things of God and ourselves."

We are *never* alone, orphaned, or in the dark. We are always in relationship with the Father, with Jesus, and with the Holy Spirit. Our lives have a profound value and significance to God, so much so that our Father provided a savior to redeem us and welcome us home.

Charles Spurgeon, one of the great religious philosophers of the 1800s, said, "Consider how precious a soul must be, when both God and the devil are after it."

If we are truly seeking the meaning of life then we must look to the verifiable script writer of life, God the Father. In Genesis 1:31 it says, "God saw everything he had made, and behold, it was very good and he validated it completely." If you believe and accept there is one true God, and His son Jesus came to forgive our sins and set the captivated free from this world's thinking, then you have resurrection power living on the inside of you. You are no longer solely carnal. You are now functioning in heavenly activity through Jesus Christ and the Holy Spirit.

God says there is more than what the eye can see and our mind can imagine. 1 Corinthians 2:9 says, "Things never discovered or heard of before, things beyond our ability to imagine these are the many things God has in store for all his lovers." We are His and we are called not to live in fear or disillusionment, but to live unashamed, confident, and unflappable in the grace and power of God.

This book is a quest to become more consciously aware of the love and presence of God in uncertain times. It's a journey to rid our lives of everyday distractions and divergences, fasting from those things that do not bring us closer to God. Some things will be obvious like certain over-indulgences in food, television time, video games, or certain reading materials. But in this book let's challenge ourselves and ask God to take us deeper in our fasting. Let Him show Himself or lack of Him in different areas of our lives that we haven't considered. I know God will have some eye-opening surprises for all of us.

The format of the book uses the twenty-one-day fast from the book of Daniel. In Daniel 10, it says for three weeks Daniel had no choice foods, no meats, no lotions. It is a fast from the luxuries and delicacies of the time. This was a fast of mourning for Daniel because he knew God's people had become lazy and indifferent and were comfortable living in obscurity and captivity. It afforded God's people certain privileges to live this way, not to stand out and to just blend in. Daniel's hopes were for restoration of godly people in a place of godlessness.

The book of Daniel is relevant today. We all have a call to live beyond what the world promotes and hold on to what is true. The challenge is to recognize we were made for so much more than the confinement of worldly motivations and concepts. We are to walk in the truth of the Father, because we are His. We are not to adopt the world's viewpoint as ours. We are spiritual beings, not just flesh and bones. As it says in James 2:26, "For as the body without the spirit is dead."

We are chosen, selected, intentional, hand-picked, determined, anointed, appointed, nominated, designed by God himself.

John 15:19 says, "I have chosen you and taken you out of the world to be mine."

1 Peter 2:9–10 Message Bible, "But you are the ones chosen by God, chosen for the high calling of priestly work, chosen to be a holy people, God's instruments to do his work and speak out for him, to tell others of the night-and-day difference he made for you—from nothing to something, from rejected to accepted.

Chapter 1: Masterpiece

Psalm 139:13–14
[13] You formed my innermost being, shaping my delicate inside and my intricate outside, and wove them all together in my mother's womb. [14] I thank you, God, for making me so mysteriously complex.

When God created you, he didn't throw his hands up in the air and say, "That's the best I can do with what I have to work with." He created you in perfect love, with details that no one could ever duplicate. We all exist as one of a kind.

I know some of us feel short-changed, but that unfortunately is the world's tunneled perspective pushing in on us.

For example, our educational system believes if a child does not learn the same way as our system prescribes, that child is branded special needs instead of our system being looked upon as deficient. The standard educational systems in the past have overlooked and labeled such great young minds as Thomas Edison and Albert Einstein, until their gifts were apparent and essential to mainstream society.

We live in a world of comparison, not cohesiveness. Yet, the Bible teaches us we are one in Christ as in 1 Corinthians 12.

> ¹³ *The old labels we once used to identify ourselves—labels like Jew or Greek, slave or free—are no longer useful. We need something larger, more comprehensive.* ¹⁴ *I want you to think about how all this makes you more significant, not less. A body isn't just a single part blown up into something huge. It's all the different-but-similar parts arranged and functioning together.*

The Bible teaches us we are selected, loved, created, wanted, and filled with purpose. We are not overlooked, overshadowed by others, or deemed worthless by our creator. What the world tries to marginalize or magnify is extraneous. What God says is, Let me overestimate you because you are my child, endowed with my presence. With God the possibilities are endless (read Matthew 19:26).

God has deliberately created you as you are for something great, wonderful, and very specific. You are significant to God beyond your wildest dreams. Because of your uniqueness, only you can contribute to the world the way He has planned, in you, through you. Yes, He can use another, but you are a preferred earthen vessel for specific tasks. Roman 12:6 says, *"We have different gifts, according to the grace given to each of us."*

We are God given, God driven.

No matter your position, age, ethnicity, gender, color, you were born, chosen for such a time as this (read Esther 4:14). You are mysteriously complex, wonderfully made, *an on-purpose person.* Even if you've been told, "I wish you weren't born" or "I don't want you in my life," your heavenly Father says to you, "This is my Masterpiece, my son, my daughter, and I rejoice over you."

> *"He will rejoice over you with gladness, He will quiet you with His love, He will rejoice over you with singing"* (Zeph. 3:17 NKJV).

The world around us is ill-equipped to see how wonderous each and every one of us has been made. Do not allow opinions of others to propel your life. You are truly a masterpiece.

> *"For we are God's workmanship, created in Christ Jesus to do good works, which God prepared in advance for us to do"* (Eph. 2:10).

Prayer

Thank you, Father, for the realization that our lives have meaning and we are not just here by accident, but we are fully present and accounted for by You, from inception to the grave. Heal the parts of us that have been fragmented by situations and circumstances. Allow us to know the fullness of our lives as preordained through Your loving craftsmanship, in Jesus's mighty name.

Chapter 2

Matthew 16:17–18
"God bless you, Simon, son of Jonah! You didn't get that answer out of books or from teachers. My Father in heaven, God himself, let you in on this secret of who I really am. And now I'm going to tell you who you are, really are. You are Peter, a rock. This is the rock on which I will put together my church, a church so expansive with energy that not even the gates of hell will be able to keep it out."

Peter is one of my favorite apostles because through the scriptures we see the evolution of Simon becoming Peter "The Rock." Peter was a vocal first responder filled with zeal but lagged behind in faith, like many of us. He had the desire, but not the know-how. We read in this verse of Matthew that Jesus doesn't even mention Peter's frailties but instead gives him a greater picture of himself. In Romans 4:17, it says, *God gives life to the dead and speaks of the nonexistent things that he has foretold and promised, as if they already existed.*

Jesus was speaking Peter "The Rock" into Simon.

Today, God is calling each and every one of us into purpose through Jesus. Surely, we can have an existence outside of God or we can have an existence with God's boundless possibilities.

The question today is what picture, what inspiration has God put in your heart, in your soul. It's there. You may have dulled it with a job that pays well or relationships that takes up some space and time, but God's purpose is still there, calling you.

In the Bible, the Book of Judges, we meet Gideon, a man who was stirred by the miracles and wonders his parents and grandparents had told him about from a different time. He realized his life lacked God's miraculous power and it stirred his heart.

When a messenger of the Lord approached Gideon and said, "God is with you, O mighty warrior," Gideon's response was doubtful. He said, "Where are all the miracle wonders? God has nothing to do with us." He was downcast and disillusioned. God didn't walk away from his people but Gideon's people had walked away from God and worshipped other Gods. The end result was there was a generation that didn't know the power of the one true God. He lived among the waywardness of his people longing for more, accepting their lack of faith and disappointment as his own fate with God.

God's belief in what he could do through Gideon was much bigger than anything Gideon imagined for himself (Judges 6). God used Gideon, calling him a warrior before he led an army. Remember, God calls things that don't yet exist as if they are real and happening in the now (Roman 4:17). God is saying, "I see you taking a victory lap, I see the strength in you that you never recognized in yourself."

We are all running a race, whether we want to admit it or not. The race of life is before us. There are fewer reasons and less despondent excuses to not succeed once you accept that God has created you for something greater. God wants a greater life for you, not a lesser life. He has given you access to all He has as the creator of the universe, through the free gift of salvation in Jesus and the boundless resources of the Holy Spirit. There is no reason for any of us to stay the same or think, "What can I possibly do," when Jesus says *all* things are possible with God (Matt. 19:26). He wants to assure us that there is a way beyond the limitations of this world and human capabilities. He, Jesus, is the way.

Prayer

Thank you for giving us the understanding that we were created for so much through you. Let us not settle for complacency over completion of purpose. Give us the fire and desire to move. When the world tells us it cannot or should not be, let us faithful know and say, "With my God all things are possible in Jesus's name."

Chapter 3

Matthew 4:2-3, 10-11
The Voice Bible
² Jesus fasted for forty days and forty nights. After this fast, He was, as you can imagine, hungry. ³ But He was also curiously stronger, when the tempter came to Jesus… **Jesus said:** *¹⁰ Get away from Me, Satan. I will not serve you. I will instead follow Scripture, which tells us to "worship the Eternal One, our God, and serve only Him." ¹¹ Then the devil left Jesus. And heavenly messengers came and ministered to Him.*

At the beginning of his ministry, Jesus spent time with his Father in prayer and fasting in order to gain spiritual strength and clarity for what was to come. Because of his time in prayer and fasting, Jesus was able to withstand every temptation that was thrown at him from the devil and was able to tell the devil to flee, without faltering. He had gained a deeper consciousness and strength spending time with the Father and letting his human desires take second place.

In Mark 9, Jesus himself speaks about prayer and fasting to his disciples. The disciples had attempted to heal a little boy of a demon that caused convulsions, but they could not. So the father of the boy pleaded to Jesus to please heal his son. Jesus commanded the demon to come out and the boy was healed.

Mark 9:28–29 Passion Bible says,

"Afterwards, when Jesus arrived at the house, his disciples asked him in private, 'Why couldn't we cast out the demon?'" [29] He answered, *"This type of powerful spirit can only be cast out by fasting and prayer."*

In the Message Bible of this account in Matthew 17, Jesus says, *"Because you're not yet taking God seriously."* In other words, no true *God sense* yet. The only way to take our Father seriously is to spend time with him and dedicate ourselves without diversions (media, busyness, distractions). The best place in this world and the next is to have the sense and the presence of God.

Jesus enjoyed company, meals, and friends. But he knew his purpose and strength would only be found in the Father's presence. Committing to prayer, with fasting from our diversions, releases breakthrough resiliency, faith, and power.

It's not a work of the flesh but a humbling resolve, a firm aim to seek God's best for us, through us.

Jesus always leads by example. He allowed himself to be baptized, he showed us how to pray and have a focused, growing relationship with the Father without interruptions and divergences

Our lives are so filled with noise, urges, and busyness, it's hard to fathom that Jesus was completely alone in a desert, led by the Holy Spirit and was tempted by the devil. (Matthew 4.1) My thought when I read this passage in Matthew is that Jesus was physically alone but did have the Holy Spirit with him. When the devil came calling with scriptures that would speak to Jesus's situation. Jesus knew clearly that evil was presenting itself as an easy way out of his circumstances. The spiritual awareness that Jesus displayed is a part of our life if we seek time and space with God.

We need to hear God's voice through the Spirit in this time, in this world. We need to take a step away from all the talking heads and distinguish what is Satan's voice and what is God's voice. That distinction will only be found in our own personal desert where we pray and ask God to reveal the truth.

Today is the day to make a commitment to pray and fast. If you are reading this, there is a reason, a purpose; God is calling you to have a deeper consciousness and spiritual awareness of the life He has planned for you. It may mean less entertainment, less news, less technology busyness but instead more prayerful cohesiveness to the Father as Jesus did.

Prayer
Thank you, Father, for allowing us to connect and focus on You through prayer and fasting. There is so much love and kindness to be done and You are our one source of all that is good. Give us the desire to draw into your presence and feed us spiritually as we fast and pray in Jesus's name.

Chapter 4

Isaiah 43:19
New International Version
*19 See, I am doing a new thing!
Now it springs up; do you not perceive it?
I am making a way in the wilderness
and streams in the wasteland.*

God gives us a new day every twenty-four hours. A new sunrise, a new sunset, and new opportunities to show His glory. As human beings, we become overly engulfed in our stressful endeavors, overwhelming circumstances, and everyday struggles that we do not realize God is at work all around us, all the time and is preparing us for a new thing. God our Father will shake things up to get us moving and paying attention to His purpose for us.

As it says in Hebrews 12:27, "The removing of those things which can be shaken." In the Message Bible, it uses the words "housecleaning…so the unshakeable essentials stand clear and uncluttered."

Anything that can be shaken is anything in which God is not in accordance with his kingdom and purpose. We must move in Christ toward God. If we dull our God-sense, we will soon allow nonsense to prevail over us and in us.

If you notice a shaking happening, it's time to take inventory of your life and call upon God for a better plan, for a refresh of His spirit. Shake off the old and let Him create a new thing inside of you.

For some of us this will be harder than others. We all have come from different circumstances, abuse, hurt, self doubt, sins, selfish motivations and mistakes. Some of these things have been imposed on us and some of us have made incorrect choices and decisions. What is impossible for you to shake off alone is completely possible with God.

Whatever and wherever the dilemma or unrest is in your life, that is where you need to let God in. Be assured you cannot have a true new beginning or restoration without a God action. If you have placed God on a shelf in any area in your life, you will never have full victory. God wants it all. As it says in Isaiah 61:3, He wants to give beauty for ashes, messages of joy instead of news of doom, and a praising heart. Pray and ask your Father to open and close doors and chip away at anything that is not of Him so you can have victory and peace in your life. No matter what past issue tries to hold you back or what messy circumstances surround you or any voices that utter you are defeated, God's promises are still true for you. Know Satan will viciously try to keep you in an old way, but God is always victorious, and He is creating a new way. The Voice Bible says in Isaiah 43:18–19, " *Don't revel only in the past or spend all your time recounting victories* **[some of us recount our defeats]** *of days going by. Watch closely I am preparing something new, it's happening now even as I speak and you're about to see it I am preparing a new way..."*

Know that your Father's intentions are always the best. I do not say this lightly as though someone had the best intentions but in the end it all worked out wrong. I say this emphatically that all goodness, all righteousness and all love is God. As people we miss the mark on all these things one time or another, but Our Father, Jesus, and The Holy Spirit never miss the mark. We can say with great assurance and no hesitation that all things work together for good for those who love the Lord (Romans 8.28). We have more than a chance we have victory in the desert, in temptations and in life itself.

Prayer

Father, we come to you knowing that You are always looking for opportunities to promote us forward through every situation and challenge. We accept that You know better and You are moving us in the right direction. Father, allow us to feel peace that surpasses understanding in all situations through the gift of the Redeemer Jesus Christ and the indwelling of the Holy Spirit with the knowledge that the best is yet to come, in Jesus's name.

Chapter 5

Romans 13:13-14
NLT

¹³ Because we belong to the day, we must live decent lives for all to see. Don't participate in the darkness of wild parties and drunkenness, or in sexual promiscuity and immoral living, or in quarreling and jealousy. ¹⁴ Instead, clothe yourself with the presence of the Lord Jesus Christ. And don't let yourself think about ways to indulge your evil desires.

God is good, merciful, and looks for ways to bless us, not suppress us. Psalm 103 gives us some of the many wonderful benefits of having a relationship with our God. We obtain forgiveness, healing, mercy, grace, unconditional love. We have the abundant life with the Father through Jesus Christ. But we must be alert to the misleadings of Satan. He tries to distract, destroy, deceive, and steal our life path through subtleties. Subtlety is one of Satan's biggest weapons. It's a thought that weaves into your conscience or subconscious. It seems to have substance, and it draws us, but if you hold it up against the Word of God, it's without merit and inferior to the promises of God. In the Garden of Eden, Eve was having a discussion with Satan, which is already a bad idea (Genesis 3). Satan speaks with her and says, *"Did God really say, 'You must not eat from this tree in the garden, and you must not touch it, or you will die.'"* Here we see Satan's ability to add uncertainty in comprehending God's words. Ambiguity is the beginning of waywardness. In Genesis 3:5, he continues by saying, *"For God knows that when you eat from it, your eyes will be opened and you will be like God, knowing good and evil.*

Satan is saying here, if you listen to me, you don't need God, you can become your own person; you can be the big decision maker; you wouldn't have to depend on God for knowledge of what is right or wrong.

Making decisions solely based on personal knowledge, feelings, and emotions are limited by one's understanding and view of the world. But there is a trustworthy voice, the creator and sustainer of the universe. He has a full picture and full understanding of all aspects of our life's journey. Satan is the subtle deceiver, but our Father is our powerful defender. Satan will try to take God out of the equation and make himself the great progressive voice. He cannot take away God's presence. God has full autonomy of all He has created.

As it says in John 10, *"The thief comes to steal and destroy."* Where he leads you will always be further away from God's best. Whether it's sexually, entertainment choices, politics, or extreme self indulgences, it will be a recipe for inner chaos and lack of peace.

We are meant to live standing with God, with obvious evidence of Him in our conduct and consciousness. The endowments of our Father's presence are restoration, peace, compassion, sound mind, direction, and most of all, eternity. These will never be reached by societal humanism. Only the originator of these hallmarks can freely give them.

To disallow any resemblance of God in our lives is to destroy the very fiber that is divine in "us." We were created in God's image (Gen 1:26). We are a part of God's divine intervention. We are his earthly vessels (2 Corin. 4:7). We are not Satan's catalysts but God's descendants. Roman 9:8 states that because of God's promise we are counted as descendants.

We must not be fooled by the elusiveness of Satan but identify pitfalls that can distract and mislead, even if it means going against the current tide.

Matthew 5:14, the Message Bible says, *"Here is another way to put it. You're here to be a light bringing out the God colors in the world. God is not a secret to be kept. We're going public with this, as public as a city on the hill. If I make you light bearers, you don't think I'm going to hide you under a bucket, do you!"*

Prayer

Father, thank you for allowing us to understand and see Satan as a subtle deceiver who only produces unrest and confusion. Father, we know through Christ that You are the same today, yesterday, and forever, always loving and wanting a relationship with us (Heb. 13:18; Deut. 31:6–8). There is no one like You. You are the alpha and the omega, the beginning and the end. All answers of life are found in You. Teach us what it means to be loved and led by You. Let us be people of hope in dark places, in Jesus's mighty name.

Study Verses
Hebrews 13:8

> *Jesus Christ is the same yesterday and today and forever. Do not be carried away by all kinds of strange teachings, for it is good for the heart to be strengthened by grace.*

Deuteronomy 31:6

> *Be strong and courageous. Do not be afraid or terrified because of them, for the Lord your God goes with you; he will never leave you nor forsake you.*

Chapter 6

In Daniel 3:16–18 of the Message Bible, King Nebuchadnezzar proclaimed, *"Who is the god who can rescue you from my power?"*

^{16–18,} Shadrach, Meshach, and Abednego answered King Nebuchadnezzar. "Your threat means nothing to us. If you throw us in the fire, the God we serve can rescue us from your roaring furnace and anything else you might cook up, O king. But even if he doesn't, it wouldn't make a bit of difference, O king. We still wouldn't serve your gods or worship the gold statue you set up."

When faced with the dilemma of doing right in the face of insurmountable odds, do we denounce what we know to be true and right only to become another part of the surface population of the silent, frozen, inactive, unnoticeable Christians? Or do we make a declaration of faith and push away the darkness even if the cost may be great? Our beliefs, our faith should be solid when we stand for what is right in God's eyes. Then there is always a path for God to work. When we shut down God's voice and his purpose, there may be no confrontation or outward conflict, but God's work through us will dwindle. In Matthew 5.16 Jesus says" *make your light shine so that others will see"*

Conflict is inevitable when you are living for Christ, but so are extraordinary possibilities and the tenacity to face and overcome challenges and powerful adversaries. Isaiah 54:17 boldly states, *"No weapon fashioned against you will succeed, and you may condemn every tongue that disputes with you. This is the heritage of the LORD's servants, whose righteousness comes from me, says the* LORD."

What we have in Christ is a new way to live. We are proactive with Christ and not reactive with the world. The world may crash down or close in around us but God has a plan, and the plan is victory and salvation. He will never leave us or forsake us.

As the three Hebrew boys faced the deadly fire of Nebuchadnezzar, they proclaimed their God is greater, and even if God didn't rescue them from the fire their lives still belonged to God, whether for the here and now or for all eternity.

There are really only three choices in our existence in our present state. Live a life void of any acknowledgment of God, live a life with some acknowledgment of God but no proven faith or power, or a life fully empowered by God with purpose and worshiping his greatness. As the book of Revelations says, you are either cold, lukewarm, or hot in your relationship with God through Christ Jesus. The acceptable position would be to have an inward and outward hot fire for Christ, and to live and do what is right in Jesus Christ through the Holy Spirit. We are to withstand the trials and troubles of this world because we know that this is not all there is and we have eternal address.

No matter what road we choose to travel, whether in the path of least resistance or the road with twists and turns, hills and valleys, and challenges, there will always be consequences. In choosing, let us choose Jesus, let us choose our Creator's way. 1 John 5:4 says, *"You see every child of God overcomes the world, for our faith is the victorious power that triumphs over the world."*

Prayer

Father, thank you for the ability to see right and wrong through Your eyes. We know You have created us and have the best plan for us. Teach us to walk away from the waywardness around us and focus directly on You and Your Word. Victory is ours only in Your presence. Compromise with the world is compromising Your truth. Enlighten us so we can be a part of Your plan of eternity for ourselves and those around us. Let our lives be a testimony of Your love, Your power. In Jesus's mighty name.

Study verse
Hebrews Amplified Bible 13:5-6

> *I will never [under any circumstances] desert you [nor give you up nor leave you without support, nor will I in any degree leave you helpless], nor will I forsake or let you down or relax My hold on you [assuredly not]! ⁶ So we take comfort and are encouraged and confidently say, "The Lord is my Helper [in time of need], I will not be afraid. What will man do to me?"*

Chapter 7

Roman 13:11
Message Bible
But make sure that you don't get so absorbed and exhausted in taking care of all your day-by-day obligations that you lose track of the time and doze off, oblivious to God.

Are you ready to live totally for God, through the example and salvation of Jesus and the power of the Holy Spirit? Are you preparing your life's testimony for your Creator? It is true we are not justified by our works, but as it says in James 2:17 *"Faith by itself if not accompanied by actions, is dead."* To paraphrase bluntly, if you are not dead then as a believer, God is not finished working through you or with you. It's time to get busy. Ask your Father: "What do you have in mind for me to do for your kingdom?"

There is a certain atmosphere of idleness around us. We sit at home on the computer or phone waiting for the coast to be clear so we can comfortably talk about Jesus with like-minded people, or worse, we follow an evangelist on television and we feel we have fulfilled our Christian obligations. Jesus was never idle or coasting. He was always preparing to do kingdom work through praying, fasting and acting out his purpose by the will of the Father.

Avoidance or idleness is not a fruit of the Holy Spirit. God's spirit is upon us to produce goodness, to build God's loving atmosphere in a fallen world. What good is our faith and our relationship with the Father if it's self-serving; only to protect and prosper us or if we isolate ourselves from unbelievers in fear of being judged or confronted.

In the Gospel of Luke, Jesus teaches a parable of the Good Samaritan to religious people who had book knowledge of Mosaic law. In this parable he shows the difference of doers of God's words and hoarders of God's words.

In Leviticus 19:18, *"The second greatest commandment is love thy neighbor as thyself."* This religious group knew this commandment but wanted an interpretation that would make them comfortable in exempting themselves from considering everyone as their neighbor. Their question was "Who is my neighbor?" At the end the parable allows them to answer their own question by asking which one of these three in the parable of the Good Samaritan (the priest, Levite, or Samaritan) acted without reservation in the commandment in Leviticus 19:18. Love thy neighbor. A lawyer in the group answered, "The one who showed him mercy."

The Samaritans, who in the eyes of the Jew were considered the least of the three passing by, acted out the true essence of the law of love. These religious leaders, who were filled with educational knowledge of God's Word, lacked heart understanding and action of God's Word. If we have knowledge of Christ, it's time to have the heart and hands of Christ.

Allow God to work through you. Our book smarts are not a great advantage to anyone except our ego. We are to unleash the power of the Word through actions.

In Luke 11, Jesus teaches us what our daily prayer should be to produce the Father's kingdom: "Your kingdom come your will be done on Earth as it is in heaven."

Read what Paul says in 2 Corinthians 15—*"Always give yourself fully to the work of the Lord because you know that your labor in the Lord is not in vain."*

We have a great commission upon us, to be God's hands of help, to be His feet, to go where called and needed, and to be His eyes, not to turn a blind eye so we don't have to take action. Let us not relinquish what has been divinely placed in us, the spirit of God. Where God leads, His light will abound. Where the world's thinking proceeds, darkness surrounds.

Study verse
1 Peter 2:9:

> *"But you are a chosen race, a royal priesthood, a holy nation, a people for his own possession, that you may proclaim the excellencies of him who called you out of darkness into his marvelous light."*

Prayer

Father, take us out of our isolation and bring us into the fullness of living for You. Let us extend ourselves with Your loving kindness and not sit by just reading Your Word, but let us be doers of the Word. Your kingdom come Your will be done on Earth as it is in heaven. Let these words be our battle cry. In heaven there is no hunger, there is no inequality, rampant abuse, greed, selfishness or hatred. Let Your kingdom come through us. Let us persevere as Your sons and daughters in Jesus's mighty name.

Chapter 8

"You, dear children, you are from God and have overcome them, because the one who is in you is greater than the one who is in the world" (1 John 4:4).

No matter what the outside climate or pressure is, God has a greater power living inside of us. God is greater than the wisest, most influential, most popular, wealthiest, highest-rated intellect in this world. He has taken residency in us to show that even though we live in the world, we are not part of the world's mindset. We were made for a higher calling and the world should not define us, contain us, or restrain us from our godly purpose. We are God's people, His tapestry to display, His glory.

Technology or "higher thinking" has not outdated us or made God obsolete. We are a people of an eternal God. Isaiah 46:10 (Message Bible) says, *"I am GOD, the only God you've had or ever will have—incomparable, irreplaceable—From the very beginning telling you what the ending will be, All along letting you in on what is going to happen, Assuring you, 'I'm in this for the long haul, I'll do exactly what I set out to do."*

God puts his resurrection power inside us so we become His springboard to all within our sphere of influence. We are to win souls to Christ. This is our great commission. To love like Jesus loves, without judgment or conditions. To adhere to the influence of the Holy Spirit that convicts us to stand up for what is right. To give glory to our heavenly Father who created us with a greater purpose than a paycheck.

We are to seek first the kingdom of God and all of its righteousness and God promises that all the rest will be added on to us (Matt. 6:33).

This is truly our warrior call, when others cower, we press in with prayer, perseverance, and a passion, knowing eternity is at stake for those around us. Many have been misled or never experienced a relationship with God through Jesus. You can be that seed of faith that makes them seek a better path.

*We are more than conquerors (*Roman 8:37). We show faith in the presence of fear. We show love to the lonely and have peace and wisdom in states of upheaval and confusion. We stand tall in God's unfailing love, not against flesh but against powers and authorities of darkness (Eph. 6:12). Let your light shine. Let your life be an example of what a difference a relationship with Jesus makes.

Prayer

Father, we thank you today for all You provide and give us, that which we never had to ask for, life and all its necessities. The sun, the air we breathe, the food we consume is all from You. Forgive us for our ungratefulness and push us forward in a thankful attitude. You have not only provided the world around us, but You have decided to reside in us. Teach us not to be selfish with the dispersing of Your love. As it is the only difference that has changed our lives, let us realize that it is the only difference that will change others' lives. Eternity is real! Lead us to pray, pursue, and love others into the reality that there will be an eternal address for each and every one of us. Your love wants everyone to come home. That is the reason for Jesus. Teach us to be Your vessels so your name is proclaimed. In Jesus's life changing mighty name

Study verse
Matthew 25, the Passion Bible

> *You have a special place in my Father's heart. Come and experience the full inheritance of the kingdom realm that has been destined for you from before the foundation of the*

world! 35 For when you saw me hungry, you fed me. When you found me thirsty, you gave me drink. When I had no place to stay, you invited me in, 36 and when I was poorly clothed, you covered me. When I was sick, you tenderly cared for me, and when I was in prison you visited.

Chapter 9

Matthew 6:10
Literal Standard Version
"Your kingdom come, Your will come to pass, as in Heaven also on the earth."

Where are you living today, God's kingdom or world's norms? Satan will try to negotiate your understanding of the kingdom of God so it seems far away and unobtainable, something that can only be a part of death. Jesus answered the question of kingdom living several times in the New Testament. In Luke 17:20–21 The Living Bible, Jesus says, *"The Kingdom of God isn't ushered in with visible signs. You won't be able to say, 'It has begun here in this place or there in that part of the country.' For the Kingdom of God is within you."*

The New International Version Bible says, "The kingdom is in your midst." If we hold this as truth spoken by Jesus in both versions then we are to live that out.

The spirit of the living God lives in us, through us, and changes the atmosphere *in our midst*.

God's kingdom, His will be done on Earth as it is in heaven is a *now* statement, not a someday in the great by and by.

Our prayers are to be filled with faith, not uncertainty like those who do not know Christ. We have a king that sits on the throne and we are a part of His kingdom. Though our prayers may be invisible words, they produce spiritual activity and visible manifestations in the natural world. Our prayer is heard by the emanating force of God Almighty, through the sacrifice of Jesus.

In Galatians 3:5, New Living Translation, Paul asks the Galatians a question: *"Does God give you the Holy Spirit and work miracles among you because you obey the law? Of course not! It is because you believe the message you heard about Christ."*

In other words, our Kingdom living is in Jesus Christ as our Lord and savior and allowing the Holy Spirit to guide us, and allow change through us, around us. Our success lies in our spiritual awareness of what Jesus did on Earth to create a home in heaven for us, not a prescribed religious doctrine or legalistic earthly standard.

We read the words of Paul in Ephesians 3: *"Now to him that is able to do exceedingly abundantly above all that we ask or think according to the power that works in us."*

We are the instruments of Christ in the now. Today is the day to live in God's Kingdom. We are to operate as warriors spiritually and physically. We are to pray before the throne as it says in Hebrews 4:16: *"Boldly unto the throne of grace."* Jesus paid an ultimate price so we could have kingdom living and spread the message that there is something more than worldly endeavors and limited governing powers. Our world is so much bigger than what our senses allow. Let's walk by faith not by sight (2 Corin. 5.7).

Study Verse
Passion Bible Matthew 6:9–13

> *"Our Beloved Father, dwelling in the heavenly realms,*
> *may the glory of your name*
> *be the center on which our lives turn.*
> *Manifest your kingdom realm,*
> *and cause your every purpose to be fulfilled on earth,*
> *just as it is in heaven.*
> *We acknowledge you as our Provider*
> *of all we need each day.*
> *Forgive us the wrongs we have done as we ourselves*
> *release forgiveness to those who have wronged us.*

*Rescue us every time we face tribulation
and set us free from evil.
For you are the King who rules
with power and glory forever. Amen.*

Prayer

Father, You are above all! Your Kingdom is what we seek. Direct us so we do not fall into temptation or evil overtake us. Let us not walk in the shadows of others, wanting what they have, but walk in the light, giving a testimony of what Jesus has done for us. For yours is the kingdom and the power and the glory *right now and forever*. In Jesus's mighty name.

Chapter 10

Joshua 1:7–8
"And don't for a minute let this Book of Revelation be out of mind. Ponder and meditate on it day and night, making sure you practice everything written in it. Then you'll get where you're going; then you'll succeed. Haven't I commanded you? Strength! Courage! Don't be timid; don't get discouraged. God, your God, is with you every step you take."

Joshua was about to lead God's people to the promised land after Moses had died. God spoke to Joshua about holding on to the Word of God handed down through Moses. Joshua needed to be courageous and focus on what God had given him to do, and not become intimidated by wavering circumstances. God promised to be his stabilizer. His unchanging standard in every situation and in every moment.

Our progress, our success, depends on our focus and who and what we trust and have confidence in. As believers we have the privilege to rise up in the morning and seek the creator of the universe before we search any worldly sources. Proverbs 8.:17 says, "Those that seek me early they will find me." With each day we have God-size possibilities and supernatural blessings available. The Bible says in Lamentations 3:23, *"Great is his faithfulness, his mercies begin afresh each morning."* As it says in Ephesians 6:13, Message Bible, *"Be prepared and take all the help you can get from God."*

We know God has complete power over any and all circumstance. Psalm 91 reminds us that God is our refuge, our home, that evil cannot get close to us...He has ordered His angels to guard us wherever we go. 1 Corinthians 10:13, Message Bible, says, *"All you need to remember is that God will never let you down; will never let you be pushed past your limit; he will always be there to help you come through."*

Our successes and spiritual awareness depend upon our relationship with God, not on the opinions of media-savvy people or limitations of a secular life. We are not to take our eyes off God's Words for our life's direction or decisions. As it says in 2 Corinthians 9:8, *"And God is able to bless you abundantly, so that in all things at all times, having all that you need you will abound in every good work."* Know who has the final victory and the last word. Our focus is forever on a higher power through prayer, praising, and absorbing God's teachings. We are not bound to the temporal, but heaven bound by God's spirit. Dwelling on circumstances or situations will only stagnant and distract us from our God-given destination. Our best handling of time is to be in constant fellowship with God. He knows what He has placed inside us—talents, wisdom—and He knows best how to use them. Trust in him; He will finish what he started.

In Philippians 1:6 (Amplified Bible) it states, *"I am convinced and confident of this very thing, that he who has begun a good work in you will continue to perfect and complete it until the day of Christ Jesus, the time of his return."*

Put your future in almighty hands by living for God every day. He is the only one who can bring you into all you can be. Our persistency and consistency only gain true success in our devotion to God alone. As David spoke in Psalms 23:4 (TPT), *"Even when your path takes me through the valley of the deepest darkest fear will never conquer me; for you already have; your authority is my strength and my peace."* Proverbs 16:20, Message Bible, says, *"It pays to take life seriously, things work out when you trust God."*

Our lives have so much meaning, but regrettably we miss it by having a casual day-to-day relationship with the world. Our Father is not superficial, and He is the only source that can add depth and profound substance to our lives. Earthly success comes to most at a detrimental cost. But as believers, our success comes through a covenant of love through the person of Jesus Christ. Only in recognizing our dependent relationship with God our Father, Jesus our Savior, and the Holy Spirit, our constant companion, can we truly be more than just conquerors, more than just successful, and more than just determined. We become glorifiers of the most high, who is boundless in all things.

Verses to ponder:
Psalm 18:30

> *"As for God, his way is perfect. The Lord's word is flawless, he shields all who take refuge in him."*

1 John 5:4 (TPT)

> *"You see, every child of God overcomes the world, for our faith is the Victorious power the triumphs over the world."*

Prayer
Father, teach us true success in You. Let our focus always to be on Your path and not the worldly meaning of success. Our accomplishments and resilience rely on You alone. As it says in Proverbs 16:33 (TPT), "We may toss a coin and roll the dice but God's will is greater than luck." Make us grounded in Your Word, in Your wisdom, and Your presence in every step and every moment, in Jesus's name.

Chapter 11

"And as for you, the anointing which you received from Him remains in you, and you have no need for anyone to teach you; but as His anointing teaches you about all things, and is true and is not a lie, and just as it has taught you, you remain in Him" (1 John 2:27).

Each one receives the anointing of the Holy Spirit at salvation. It comes in us from the moment we trusted Christ for our salvation. The price for this anointing and indwelling of the Holy Spirit was bought and paid for in full by the precious blood of Jesus Christ.

We have such a privilege to be called sons and daughters, born again in Christ (John 3:3). Of course, we learn from others and our own mistakes. But if we apply the Word of God and pray, we can learn and discern what is from God or not.

We have the great privilege to continue the work of Jesus.

Jesus said before he departed from his earthly body (John 14:12), *"Very truly I tell you, whoever believes in me will do the works I have been doing, and they will do even greater things than these because I am going to the Father."* Notice the last part because he is going to the Father, which completed our anointing to do His work. In John 14:13, Jesus further says, *"And I will do whatever you ask in my name so that the Father may be glorified in the son."*

We are equipped and anointed for the work of the Lord because Jesus has made it so. In 1 John 2:27 NIV, it says, *"But* the anointing teaches you about all things, and as the anointing is real, not counterfeit."

A spirit-filled life is a part of our inheritance and evident in our lives. (Eph. 4) "He handed out gifts above and below, filled heaven with his gifts, filled the earth with his gifts…to train Christ's followers in skilled servant work."

Abiding in Jesus means the resurrection power is a real and active in us and allows us to show Jesus to others. To deny the reality of the spirit working in us and through us is to deny what His death and resurrection has accomplished, life of abundance, beyond the here and now and unmerited forgiveness for all who accept Jesus. *"I came that they may have life and have it in abundance"* (John 10:10).

Jesus is saying you are the movement of God, I am giving you the Holy Spirit and greater things you will do then I did because I sit at my Father's right hand and you have been raised in me. We are…love in action, truth seekers…spirit-filled wise in this hour. Do not take God's anointing for granted.

Peter enthusiastically prayed after he and John were released from prison for preaching and healing in the name of Jesus. It was bold and uncompromising. Acts 4:30–31,

> *"Stretch out Your hand to cure and to perform signs and wonders through the authority and by the power of the name of Your holy Child and Servant Jesus. ³¹ And when they had prayed, the place in which they were assembled was shaken; and they were all filled with the Holy Spirit, and they continued to speak the Word of God with boldness.* Let our faith be vivid and uncompromising in the world, so others may be drawn to Christ."

Verses to ponder:
1 Corinthians 12:7,

> *"Each believer is given continuous Revelation by the Holy Spirit to benefit not just himself but all."*

1 Corinthians 12:27,

> *"You are the body of the Anointed One, and each of you is unique and vital part of it."*

Colossians 3:1,

> *"If then you have been raised with Christ, seek the things that are above, where Christ is, seated at the right hand of God. Set your minds on things that are above, not on things that are on earth. For you have died, and your life is hidden with Christ in God. When Christ who is your life appears, then you also will appear with him in glory."*

Prayer

Father, thank you for Your Holy Spirit, it is the same spirit that presided in Peter and John, that allowed them to speak boldly and heal in Jesus's name. It is the same spirit that was physically deposited upon Jesus at his baptism by John. It is the same spirit that rose Jesus from the dead, *that resurrection power*. Teach us to live in the fullness of the anointing of Holy Spirit and to express Your truth and love boldly, in Jesus's mighty.

Chapter 12

Luke 9:1–5
The Message Bible
"Jesus called the twelve and gave them authority and power to deal with all the demons and cure diseases. He commissioned them to preach the news of God's kingdom and heal the sick. He said, "Don't load yourselves up with equipment. Keep it simple; you are the equipment. And no luxury inns—get a modest place and be content there until you leave. If you're not welcomed, leave town. Don't make a scene. Shrug your shoulders and move on."

Keep it simple! That's Jesus's call. The most important part is whose authority you are working under. Think about the simple truth of Jesus's ministry in Matthew 22:37–40. Message *bible Jesus said, "'Love the Lord your God with all your passion and prayer and intelligence.' This is the most important, the first on any list. But there is a second to set alongside it: 'Love others as well as you love yourself.' These two commands are pegs; everything in God's Law and the prophets hang from them."*

To love and humble ourselves before the Father allows him to work through us. To love others as ourselves is to be aware of others' physical, mental, and spiritual conditions and reach out our hands and prayers to show God's love.

The *only* resource you need is a relationship with the Father, the Son, and the Holy Spirit.

You don't need a wooden podium, or beautiful outfits, or the right position in society, you need to express the love and light of God. Travel with the light of God and be a light to others.

Kingdom life is about bearing good fruit, abiding in Jesus. In John 15, Jesus says, *"If you abide in me and my voice abides in you, everything you ask will come to pass for you. Your abundant growth, in your faithfulness as my followers, will bring glory to the father."* To experience this blessing, we must be followers of Christ.

First, it's about our connection to Christ, then we will have substance (fruit) in our walk, which will produce the beauty of God's kingdom around us and in us.

As Jesus states in Matthew 18, *"I tell you the truth, whatever you forbid on earth will be forbidden in heaven, and whatever you permit on earth will be permitted in heaven."* We are in the best company we can be in, with heaven on our side.

Prayer

Heavenly Father, I come before You today and thank You for the many blessings and opportunities of serving You and serving others. Let me always remember You are my power source. You light up the dark places and make the crooked path straight. I know because of Your great love that no weapon formed against me will prosper or overtake me. You are the alpha and omega, the first and final word, You alone are my vine and I am the branch. In You I will abide, in Jesus's mighty name.

Chapter 13

Psalm 144
*I Praise the Lord, who is my rock.
He trains my hands for war
and gives my fingers skill for battle.*

As believers of the New Testament, we have an idea that Jesus was just kind, gentle and loving, which is true. We forget that he came to wage a battle against the devil in every arena, strongholds, infirmities, lawlessness, hypocrisy, and most important, in our very soul.

He didn't try to blend in or conform to the hierarchy of the religion or government of the time. Instead, he came to start a fire in us. In Luke 12 (Message Bible), Jesus says, *"Do you think I came to smooth things over and make everything nice? Not so. I've come to disrupt and confront!"* You might be saying, "Wait, didn't Jesus say we would have peace?"

In John 14:27 (Amplified Bible), Jesus says, *"Peace I leave with you; My perfect peace I give to you; not as the world gives do I give to you. Do not let your heart be troubled, nor let it be afraid. Let My perfect peace calm you in every circumstance and give you courage and strength for every challenge."*

Jesus has equipped us to fight the good fight (1 Tim. 6:12). This a champion statement. We are to know the truth through God's Word and not be complacent and allow evil to prevail. We know through scriptures that King David before every battle, sought the Lord and Jesus, before every dawn, sought the Father.

We are also to seek God before we ensue the battle every day.

Our greatest strategies will be on our knees, and our hands lifted toward Heaven. Paul says in 2 Corinthians 10:4 (the Voice), *"The weapons of the war we're fighting are not of this world but are powered by God and effective at tearing down the strongholds erected against His truth."*

We walk in victory with the path forward that God has laid out, praising his mighty name. In 2 Chronicles 20, God laid out his battle plan. *"The Lord said: 'Be not afraid or dismayed at this great multitude, for the battle is not yours, but God's. Go down against them tomorrow,'...the people rose in the morning walking into battle singing, 'Praise and give thanks to the Lord, for His mercy and lovingkindness endure forever.'"* The battle was already won before they even marched because they trusted God and moved toward the fight.

Don't hide from the battle, don't pretend it's not your battle, and by no means don't surrender for a lesser purpose than "fighting the good fight of faith." God does expect you to march forward and let His light shine through you and around you. We are not to downplay God's influence through us but uphold and surrender to His presence in us. Our position should never be what can I do, but Lord, what would you have me do through your spirit"

Verses to ponder:
Romans 8:31

"If God is for us, who can be against us?"

Hebrews 12.1 Message Bible
Discipline in a Long-Distance Race

"Do you see what this means—all these pioneers who blazed the way, all these veterans cheering us on? It means we'd better get on with it. Strip down, start running—and never quit! No extra spiritual fat, no parasitic sins. Keep your eyes on Jesus, who both began and finished this race we're in. Study how He did it. Because He never lost sight

of where He was headed—that exhilarating finish in and with God—He could put up with anything along the way: Cross, shame, whatever. And now He's there, in the place of honor, right alongside God. When you find yourselves flagging in your faith, go over that story again, item by item, that long litany of hostility He plowed through. That will shoot adrenaline into your souls."

Prayer

Thank you, Father, for your grace, as you told Paul in 2 Corinthians 9, "My grace is sufficient for you, for my power is made perfect in weakness." Therefore, I will boast all the more gladly about my weaknesses, so that Christ's power may rest on me. Teach me, Lord, to proceed forward and not stand on the sidelines, but give me Your protection and knowledge to move in Your kingdom in Jesus's name.

Chapter 14

Matthew 13:31
"Heaven's kingdom realm can be compared to the tiny mustard seed that a man takes and plants in his field. Although the smallest of all the seeds, it eventually grows into the greatest of garden plants, becoming a tree for the birds to come and build their nests in its branches."

Zechariah 4:10
"Do not despise these small beginnings, for the Lord rejoices to see the work begin."

Maybe as a Christian you have been dormant in response to Jesus's great commission. Maybe you have been busy with work, family, or everyday life. Today is your day of small beginnings. Ask your heavenly Father to open your eyes and heart to operate in His Holy Spirit as the early Christians did.

I know someone reading this may say, "I cannot just go up to strangers and start praying for them or talk about Jesus." You can, however, pray for those in your path and show Jesus to others in your everyday behavior. As quoted by Francis of Assisi, "Preach the gospel at all times, When necessary, use words."

In Zechariah 4.10, *"Don't despise small beginnings,"* was written in reference to rebuilding the temple that was in ruins. Many at that time felt this tedious task was insignificant and too overwhelming. They saw there was too much to do and too little know-how in them.

Some of us may have adopted this same attitude about the world we live in. It has too many moving parts, too many enemies, too many unbelievers. But God is in the rebuilding and restoration business, so every knee-bending and arm-raised position is a warrior stance that leads us into the reconstruction business for God.

In Zechariah 4:6, God says to Zerubbabel who he commanded to begin the rebuilding: *"Your strength and prowess will not be enough to finish My temple, but My Spirit will be."* And God says to those coming against Zerubbabel's efforts to rebuild the temple: (Zechariah 4:7) *"Who are you, O mighty mountain of opposition? Before Zerubbabel, you will become nothing more than a smooth plain, and he will quarry the capstone."*

Our mustard seed prayer and the Word of God is our protection, our projection, and our correction in our doubt. We have already won if we are standing with God in Jesus.

Our small beginning is the path God has deliberately set in front of us. Our families, our community, our country, all is being tethered by the power of God in us, through us, and around us.

There are no unacknowledged prayers to an all-knowing God, and there are no minor requests to an unlimited God. Praying, seeking, and trusting God constantly in all will alleviate confusion and stress, because you will know God is in control. There is a Hebrew expression, "Im Yirtzeh Hashem," meaning, If God Wills It. The expression is a resolve that in the smallest occurrences to the largest state of affairs, we are always in the hands of the Almighty from daybreak to sunset. In allowing God to work in casual everyday occurrences, and in large on-purpose gatherings is the providence or serendipity of a believer's life. There truly are no insignificant starts because *all things work together for good for those who love the Lord* (Romans 8:28).

In chapter 1 of this book, I quoted Psalm 139:13, *"You shaped me first inside then out; you formed me in my mother's womb."* As a masterpiece of God almighty, you have been born into a society, a culture for God's purpose, in God's time. Don't neglect your seed. It was placed in you by God, and don't despise your small beginnings…just begin.

Verses to ponder:
Genesis 50:20, New Heart Bible

> *"As for you, you meant evil against me, but God turned it into good in order to bring about this present result, to save the lives of many people.*

Psalm 33:11, Passion Translation

> *"His destiny-plan for the Earth stands sure his forever-plan remains in place and will never fail."*

Prayer

Father, thank you for the knowledge that You are always with us and we have nothing to fear and we have every promise in the Bible to be refreshed by. Our small or tedious beginnings will lead us to Your glorious outcome. Teach us to walk in faith and obedience and not waver from our purpose, especially in confrontations. Let us stand on solid ground through our everlasting relationship with You, in Jesus's mighty name.

Chapter 15

Titus 1:2-4, The Message
My aim is to raise hopes by pointing to the way to life without end. This is the life God promised long ago—and He doesn't break promises. I've been entrusted to proclaim this message by order of our Savior. Receive everything God our Father and Jesus our Savior give you!

What a friend we have in Jesus! In the New Testament, we see the Father's intentions through Jesus of redemption, love, miracles, and spiritual awareness throughout Jesus and his encounters. These spiritual covenant promises remain intact and even greater in us upon his earthly departure (to sit at the right hand of the Father, Luke 22:69). The promises of the Bible are meant for the here and now and to carry into the next generation and then eternity. In Isaiah 59:21 it is written, *"This is My covenant promise to them: My Spirit, which rests on and moves in you, and My words, which I have placed within you, will continue to be spoken among you and move you to action. And not only you, but so it will be for your children and their children too. And so on through the generations for all time."*

This is such a strong declaration, a glorious unfolding of our lives that effect generations to come straight into eternity.

Unfortunately, as human beings we get so involved in our solo life that we forget our lives are indeed forever connected and our decisions are more far reaching than just here and now.

The well-known historian Kevin Kruse of Princeton University said, "Life is about making an impact, not making an income. Nothing tangible is permanent. No work lasts forever! Technology changes, businesses falter, and societies crumble. Compare this truth to God and His work. Every work and Word of God stands and has eternal impact. God's Word is not self-serving, it's not about being perfect! It's not even about putting your best effort forward to gain a worldly reward. We are made for so much more. In this world with all its beauty, goodness, and captivations, it's still not as good as it gets. There is something more, something holy that this world will never satisfy.

This something is the same something that changed Saul to Paul. Paul gave up every earthly pursuit and status to share the goodness of God and the redemption found through Jesus Christ. Instead of feeling displaced for no longer having a high status esteemed by important people, he felt blessed, loved, and at peace with no regret for what he left behind. In Philippians 3:7–8, Paul says, *"Yet all of the accomplishments that I once took credit for, I've now forsaken them and I regard it all as nothing compared to the delight of experiencing Jesus Christ as my Lord! To truly know him meant letting go of everything from my past and throwing all my boasting on the garbage heap. It's all like a pile of manure to me now, so that I may be enriched in the reality of knowing Jesus Christ and embrace him as Lord in all of his greatness."*

Our busy lifestyles will never satisfy our spiritual side. We can be like Martha in the Gospel of Luke, running around making grand preparations and grand gestures, or be like Mary (Martha's sister), who simply wanted to know the ways of God through Jesus. In Luke 10:41-42, the Lord speaks to Martha about her busyness. *"Martha, my beloved Martha. Why are you upset and troubled, pulled away by all these many distractions? Are they really that important? [42] Mary has discovered the one thing most important by choosing to sit at my feet. She is undistracted, and I won't take this privilege from her."*

We all have the same privilege as Mary—to sit in Christ's presence and draw strength, peace, and wisdom. Our perpetual movement matters little to Christ if it is void of the love of the

Father. The same Father-God who gave up his son Jesus, so He could make a home in heaven for us. Let us reattached ourselves to our source of everything, and detach from the busyness that leads nowhere.

Verses to ponder:
Proverbs 3:6

> *"In all your ways submit to the Lord, and he will make your path straight."*

Psalm 115:1–2

> *"Not for our sake, but for your name's sake, show your glory. Do it on account of your merciful love. Do it on account of your faithful ways."*

Prayer

Father, we thank you for Your eternal presence. There is never a day where You are not available through Jesus and the Holy Spirit. You refresh us, You comfort us, and You direct us. Let our wisdom and deeds be designated and prescribed by You, so they have an eternal impact for those around us and our lives ahead of us. As it says in Psalm 23:6, Passion Translation, "For your goodness and love pursue me all the days of my life. Then afterward, when my life is through, I will return to your glorious presence to be forever with you." Let my life be Your example of Your love, in Jesus's name.

Chapter 16

Message Bible
"God's promise"
I will answer them before they even call to me.
While they are still talking about their needs,
I will go ahead and answer their prayers! (Isa. 65:24)

God is looking to place his favor upon us. The only request He has of you is to live the life He has given, fully and committed to Him through Jesus.

Many of us come from a belief system that God is waiting to punish us for our wrongdoings, just waiting to point out our evil ways. Some of us may even believe we must perform some ritualistic "jump through hoops" task in order to gain the Father's mercy, grace, and favor. The Word of God teaches us the only way to come is *as we are*, with bumps, bruises, and burdens. In Luke 15:20–2, the parable of the Prodigal Son, we see the favor and grace of God our Father. *"When he (the son) was still a long way off, his father saw him. His heart pounding, he ran out, embraced him, and kissed him. The son started his speech: 'Father, I've sinned against God, I've sinned before you; I don't deserve to be called your son ever again.'"* The next verse shows how deep the love of the Father is. He doesn't even care to acknowledge the son's wrongdoings. Verse 22–24 *"But the father wasn't listening. He was calling to the servants, 'Quick. Bring a clean set of clothes and dress him. Put the family ring on his finger and sandals on his feet. Then get a prize-winning heifer and roast it. We're going to feast! We're going to have a wonderful time! My son is here—given up for dead and now alive! Given up for lost and now found!' And they began to have a wonderful time."*

It is hard for us to fathom that before we even formulate a prayer or officially ask for forgiveness, it's as good as done in God's kingdom. There is no process or prescription you have to follow, such as "say five of these prayers," or a checklist of things to do before God even considers your prayer. God's mercy is free and always available through the acceptance of Jesus. In 1 John 3.1, it says, *"What marvelous love the Father has extended to us! Just look at it—we're called children of God! That's who we really are."*

We have a blessed assurance that *nothing can separate us from the love of God* (Rom. 8:39). *He is always willing to accept a contrite heart.* Psalms 51:17 states, *"God will not reject a broken and repentant heart."*

The reality is, long before one of our days came to be, God chose each and every one of us into existence, to be loved by Him. Giving us breath and life was and is His good pleasure. Knowing He loved us first, how could we ever think He would want to walk away from His beloved.

In Isaiah 30:18, the Word professes, *"For this reason the Lord is still waiting to show his favor to you so he can show you his marvelous love. He waits to be gracious to you. He sits on his throne ready to show mercy to you."*

If we have become wayward in any area, bring it before the Lord. There is no condemnation but grace and mercy. Lamentations 3 reminds us that *God's compassions, his mercies, are new every single morning.* Each day we have the opportunity to start fresh and ask His forgiveness and walk in His will for us. As the Psalmist says in 139:23–24, *"Search me O God, know my heart try me, know my thoughts and see if there be any wicked way in me and leave me in the way of everlasting."*

Whatever worldly lifestyle, mindset, or preference in any area of your life that lacks God's presence, confess it. God offers something far greater than you can imagine, far greater than what you have settled for. Let His blessings, favor, mercies, and forgiveness flow. Before you finish your prayer, He is preparing a better outcome.

The true essence of our relationship with our Father is simple. God doesn't want something from us, He simply wants us (C. S. Lewis). The proof is in the sacrifice of His only begotten son Jesus.

Verses to ponder:
Joshua 1:5, WEB

> *"I will not fail you nor forsake you."*

Ezekiel 34:16, WEB

> *"I will seek that which was lost, and will bring back that which was driven away, and will bind up that which was broken, and will strengthen that which was sick."*

Prayer
Thank you, Father, for patiently waiting for us to return to You. You are our Creator, Our Father, Our first love. Teach us to have a deep abiding relationship with You. You have blessed us with so much, not because we are entitled or worthy, but because You first loved us. Thank you for holding a steadfast vigil over us and hearing our prayers. We know as it says in Jeremiah 42, "You are with us and will save us." You will show us compassion in Jesus's mighty name. Amen.

Chapter 17

Galatians 5:13–26
The Message Bible
13–15 It is absolutely clear that God has called you to a free life. Just make sure that you don't use this freedom as an excuse to do whatever you want to do and destroy your freedom. Rather, use your freedom to serve one another in love; that's how freedom grows. For everything we know about God's Word is summed up in a single sentence: Love others as you love yourself. That's an act of true freedom. If you bite and ravage each other, watch out—in no time at all you will be annihilating each other, and where will your precious freedom be then?

God created us and allows us to exist and experience freedom. John 8:36 states, *"Whom the son sets free is free indeed."*

The rules and regulations of society and even religion are an indoctrination of ideologies that produce habits or acceptable patterned behaviors. If you follow the rules, you are a part of the culture, the party, the club, et cetera. If you don't follow the common philosophy, you are neutralized, abandoned, and canceled. In God's plan there is no dissociation, alienation, abandonment. In the world's progressive philosophy, you walk a tightrope, thinking you are walking carefully on that acceptable thin line, and suddenly someone changes the rules and you are the collateral damage of someone else's new mindset. That is not freedom and that is definitely not how God deals with us. If that was how God dealt with us, we would all cease to exist forever. Because He doesn't want eternity without us, He gave a sacrifice, His son Jesus, so we only had to accept the sacrifice to come home to heaven.

Life will produce hills and valleys and shaky ground, but we do not walk on eggshells before our loving Father, for His love always accepts us. He accepts our apologies and allows us to begin again. Our free will is our instrument of choosing for Him and gives us the ability to choose what is pleasing to God. The relationship between God and His people is soul awakening, not a mindless bogging down of legalistic associations or ritualistic indoctrinations.

In Jeremiah 29:13 AMP, it says, *"Then [with a deep longing] you will seek Me and [you will] find Me when you search for Me with all your heart."* As it says in Hebrews 13:5, *God will never leave you or abandon you.* You will never receive a pink slip from God; He won't unfriend you, and He will never distant himself from you. He is unconditional and constant love.

There is a heart choice to be made, not a dogma to follow. Anything less than making a conscious decision is dismantling our gift of free will. Disassembling our freedom has never been and will never be an act of God but an act of earthly pressure. It is an act of creating a fear-bound, spiritless, self-serving people that will follow what is fed to them because freedom has been minimized or stripped in the society in which they live.

Hosea 4:6 states, *"My people are destroyed for a lack of knowledge."* As Jesus says in John 8:32, *"You will know the truth and the truth will set you free."* We have choices. We have impossible possibilities. We do not have to follow the crowd blindly or be held to worldly rulers who try to maintain their position of power. Tune into the only human being who came so He could bring you home—Jesus. He was and is an example of truthful discourse and respect for those who are seeking answers. In fact, Jesus usually spoke in parables, in-depth exchanges so He could start a thought process. Never did He force feed doctrine or take away the ability to reason out. Jesus saw people as valuable and their questions, their voices, important. He knew sharing the truth and demonstrating love would transform lives. With no other agenda but love, Jesus set us free from a life of sin and fear and gave purpose instead of aimless pursuits. *"I came so that everyone would have life and have it to the fullest"* (John 10:10).

We live in a culture of constant power struggles. The tools of our world are placation to those whom we believe are powerful. We express provocation toward those that do not follow. We are increasingly used to silencing and eliminating viewpoints contrary to the accepted narrative. We have lost so much ability to challenge the veracity of the media, government, economics, modern medicine, or ritualistic activities, even when we know it is not God's best for us. The trajectory of our lives is being propelled or defined by external sources that subjugate us into what life should be according to the self-imposed ruling class. If we give ourselves over to the viewpoint and power of the world, we will be forever beholding and enslaved by our external conditions and circumstances. God is an internal source that provides stability, peace, love, freedom, and unshakeable truth for those who seek Him. He changes our hearts; he doesn't creates new laws.

In Ezekiel 36:26, it says, *"I will plant a new heart and new spirit inside of you. I will take out your stubborn, stony heart and give you a willing, tender heart of flesh."* The only experience that will change you and give you total freedom is true unconditional love, which only comes from the Father through Jesus. Don't devalue what God has done by following the crowd blindly but engage and search for your God through the example and saving grace of Jesus and the leading of the Holy Spirit. God welcomes a seeking heart. You don't need a crowd behind you or in front of you. You just need a one-on-one relationship with Jesus.

Verses to ponder:
1 Chronicles 16:11, *"God-seekers, be jubilant! Study God and his strength, seek his presence day and night."*

Prayer
Father, thank you for always being there, providing truth and a discerning mind to reason. Let Your spirit guide us in this world where opinions are taken as truth and truth is looked at as an

absurdity. Fill us with Your knowledge and understanding so we may show Your love and shine Your light in the darkest of places, in the hardest of times. Don't let our hearts grow weary or indifferent to Your truth. Keep us alert and ever diligent in loving You and loving others. Thank you for the security of Your love that sets us free. Thank you for the genuine reality of eternal life that drives us to share this truth with others. All this in Jesus's name.

Chapter 18

1 Corinthians 15:58
The Passion Translation
"So now, beloved ones, stand firm, stable, and enduring. Live your lives with an unshakeable confidence. We know that we prosper and excel in every season by serving the Lord, because we are assured that our union with the Lord makes our labor productive with fruit that endures."

Can we really fathom who our Father is, the sovereign creator of all, or Jesus, our Savior who has secured our eternal destiny by His own free will, and accepted our punishment, or the Holy Spirit, our spiritual consciousness and helper, who brings kingdom living to the earth in us, through us. We have the A-team with us. Knowing who stands with us, who can be against us? God himself has promoted us for His good purpose (Rom. 8:31).

We have a higher love behind us, in us, through us. It's a love that says, "I know you are not perfect, but you are perfectly loved." That kind of love can only come from one who wanted you to exist. The originator of all things created, including a one-of-a-kind original you.

We are born to receive His purpose, His love, and His kingdom. We need to recognize that it is not a self-journey to unravel, but a God journey to be filled with His good purpose. I love the way Romans 5:6–8 in the Message Bible states this: *"He didn't and doesn't wait for us to get ready. He presents himself for this sacrificial death when we were too weak and rebellious to do anything to get ourselves ready."* God put His love on the line for us while offering His son in a sacrificial death while we were of no use whatever to Him (sinners).

Yes, indeed, there is a life to live with struggles and troubles but not without divine help or outcome. *Isaiah 43:2 states, "When you pass through [a] the deep, stormy sea, you can count on me to be there with you. When you pass through raging rivers, You will not drown. When you walk through persecution like fiery flames, you will not be burned; the flames will not harm you."*

We have an undeniable purpose, each and every one of us. If we trust in our Father Almighty's provision, we will prosper in what is set before us.

> Psalm 1:3
> *They are strong, like a tree planted by a river.*
> *The tree produces fruit in season,*
> *and its leaves don't die.*
> *Everything they do will succeed.*

We have a three-fold connection to the kingdom of God the Father, Jesus, and the Holy Spirit. We are on the winning side of eternity. Let us not for one second believe that Satan has gotten the better of us, because the worst part of us has already been washed clean by the blood of the Lamb. There is no waiting for God to show up. He is already here and always will be. He is waiting upon us to humble ourselves in all areas and trust in His ways and not in our human philosophies.

Verses to ponder:
Ephesians 1:20–23 (Message Bible)

> *"Let us remember God raised him (Jesus) from death and set him on a throne in deep heaven, in charge of running the universe, everything from galaxies to governments, no name and no power exempt from his rule. And not just for the time being, but forever. He is in charge of it all, has the final word on everything. At the center of all, Christ rules*

the church. The church, you see, is not peripheral to the world; the world is peripheral to the church. The church is Christ's body, in which he speaks and acts, by which he fills everything with his presence."

Prayer

Heavenly Father, thank you for creating us with the capacity to realize we need something greater than self-motivation to make sense of our short life here. We toil to do good in our own strength way too many times when our resilience and power should be found in you. Let us always remember we have the A-Team with us and our self-power is no match for Your divine intervention, which is around us every day.

Lord, let us not forget we are the church meant to perpetuate the goodness of God through Jesus Christ in the help of the Holy Spirit. In Jesus's mighty name!

Chapter 19

Joshua 24:15, *"But if serving the Lord seems undesirable to you, then choose for yourselves this day whom you will serve. …But as for me and my household, we will serve the Lord."*

Who are you serving? It's a question that needs to be asked in every aspect of our lives. The next question is, who are taking along with you? Someone is always watching and following your example, your decisions. We influence people purposely and fortuitously.

In the above passage, Joshua makes a very poignant point that, no matter what, we will follow something. The choices will always be God or something else, not God or nothing. For us to believe that we can conduct life on our own terms and be fully resolved in the matter is self-delusional. There will always be something missing. Our comprehension of how to run our life or follow what is the popular reasoning is flawed. It's like running up the down escalator stairs facing backward. You cannot see where you're going, but you know there is movement and you are going somewhere. God gives a pathway and tells you exactly where your destination will be. John 3:16 says, *"For God so loved the world that he gave his only son, that whoever believes in him shall not perish but have eternal life."* Eternity is your destination.

In Deuteronomy 30, *Moses gives his farewell speech to the Israelites as they are about to embark into the promised land. It goes as follows: "This day I call the heavens and the earth as witnesses against you that I have set before you life and death, blessings and curses. Now choose life, so that you and your children may live and that you may love the Lord your God, listen to his voice, and hold fast to him. For the Lord is your life, and he will give you many years in the land he swore to give to your fathers, Abraham, Isaac, and Jacob."*

God is the advocate for life more abundantly (John 10:10). If you choose anything less, you have cheated yourself. Jerry Garcia, American songwriter and singer said, "Constantly choosing the lesser of two evils is still choosing evil." There are only two choices before us. God's plan or everything that leads us away from God. If we turn away from God, we are losing sight of His boundless love, promises, and the rest of eternity with Him. Unfortunately, our scope of considerations and motivations are very earthbound and somewhat fear driven. Many believe they would miss out on the human experience by aligning with God. It is just the opposite. We will enjoy the fullness of life through the creator of life. Also, in choosing a godly life, we are exhibiting a longer view of life that does not contain itself to this world alone and lights a pathway for generations to come.

If we denounce and deter from the ways of God, our children's children will be wandering in an abyss of lack, not having knowledge of right and wrong. They will be easily swayed by social practices and social mores that lead nowhere. In Leviticus 10:3, Moses says, *"To the one who comes near me I will show myself holy before all the people I will show my glory."* Our lives are worth so much more than what our worldly short-sightedness allows us to see. Come near to God and allow His glory to overflow through you.

The Message Bible in Matthew 7:13–14 says it like this: *"Don't look for shortcuts to God. The market is flooded with surefire, easygoing formulas for a successful life that can be practiced in your spare time. Don't fall for that stuff, even though crowds of people do. The way to life—to God!—is vigorous and requires total attention."*

God wants a definitive I CHOOSE LIFE; I CHOOSE YOU FATHER!

He allowed a savior to show us our way home and has given us an all-knowing loving spirit that chooses to dwell within us to further align us with Him. All this to show us how deep the love of the Father goes, and how His provision is all around us, even in us. God pursued us first. Choosing Him is a privilege He gave us. As it says in 1 John 4:19, *"We love because he first loved us."* And in Colossians 3:12, *"You are always and dearly loved by God! So robe yourself with virtues of God, since you have been divinely chosen to be holy."* We have nothing to brag or boost about in finding our way to our Father. We are His, created by His hands. Our sincere response without hesitation should be, *"For me and my household shall follow the Lord."*

Verses to ponder:
Psalm 33:11, the Passion Bible

> *"His destiny-plan for the earth stands sure. His forever-plan remains in place and will never fail."*

Psalm 100:3, The Passion Bible

> *"And realize what this really means—we have the privilege of worshiping Yahweh our God. For he is our Creator and we belong to him. We are the people of his pleasure."*

Prayer
Heavenly Father, thank you for always being aware of our human condition but not allowing us to accept it as our gospel. You have provided a kingdom gospel that is greater than any earthly understanding or force created by human minds or hands. We live in Your sovereignty, in Your kingdom, in Your will, on earth as it is in heaven. Teach us to walk in Your ways and prepare the way of the Lord, in Jesus's mighty name.

Chapter 20

Exodus 17:15
New Living Translation
"Moses built an altar there and named it Yahweh-Nissi" (which means "the LORD is my banner").

Banners and flags are identifiers. They rally people physically, ideologically, and spiritually. They demonstrate certain common kinship and connection. They display a belief system and a certain loyalty.

In the Bible, banners are used in same manner as mentioned above. They display God's devotion to us and our connection to God.

In the above passage, Exodus 17, the banner is a symbol of God's leadership, protection, and intervention on behalf His beloved people. In Psalm 60:6 (NABRE), it is a testimony of worship of who we belong to. "Raise up a banner for those who revere you." In Psalm 20:5, the banner is victory and praise, *"We will shout for joy when you are victorious and we will lift up our banners in the name of God." In* Song of Solomon 2:4, the banner is provision and comfort: *"He led me to the banquet room and showered me with love."*

The banners in the Bible express our personal access, dependence, and relationship with God. God holds complete sovereignty, love, faithfulness, and redemption under His banner. These characteristics of the Almighty's banner cannot be altered. God is and will forever be the standard for all that is good. We are His church;

His banner over us is love. As Jesus said in Matthew 16:18, *"The gates of hell will not prevail against the church [his people]."* His protection, grace, and love are undeniable and unshakeable. *God is love and love never fails* (Corin. 13:8). In Isaiah 59:19, we read God's promise to those who revere Him. *"When the enemy shall come in like a flood, the spirit of the Lord shall lift up a standard against him."*

There may be tens of thousands of opinions, campaigns, and fluctuations in the world's idea of right and wrong, good and evil, but the truth is God's banner. His standards will prevail no matter what comes against them. In Isaiah 55:11, Message Bible, Isaiah the prophet proclaims the power of God, *"So will the words that come out of my mouth not come back empty-handed. They will do the work I sent them to do. They will complete the assignment I gave them."*

So many have chosen not to have any association or belief in a sovereign God. There have been some concessions made toward this narrative. Prayer has been eliminated from many institutions. Universities promote the idea that anything from the Bible is archaic. Even churches feel pressure to change their message to accommodate our society. There even was a movement to remove "In God we Trust" from our currency. The process is aimed at reducing or lessening the representation of God from society. Eliminating God's influence so we can become autonomous and reconsider and reestablish what is moral versus immoral is like pretending you are a doctor so you can operate on people and feel in control of their destiny. This mindset is totally self-centered and void of knowledge. C. S. Lewis said, "A man can no more diminish God's glory by refusing to worship him then a lunatic can put out the Sun by scribbling the word Darkness on the walls of his cell." God's banner and all it contains for us will always be, even when we refuse to give God a second thought. Every blade of grass, every sunset, every breath of air, every starry sky, and every newborn's cry, will always shout there is something greater than us. The greatest human mind cannot fathom our true origin of existence or the continued sustaining of life on a planet that is oddly perfectly formed for human survival. This earth continues without ceasing from generation to generation. Truly there is no input from us on the sun rising or a storm brewing. We are only spectators trying to control the wind and rain, in hopes that we are mightier than the elements.

One of the greatest minds of our time, Albert Einstein, said, "There are only two ways to live your life. One is as though nothing is a miracle, and the other is as though everything is a miracle."

Examine the banner you are carrying today. What does it display? If the cause you rally behind is the limited self-absorption of your or someone else's "thinking" or it doesn't prompt you or others to a greater consciousness beyond yourself, it will fall flat and will not have any lasting goodness. If it is selfish and not selfless, it is a pit that you are dragging yourself and others into. It will have no true meaning, just raw emotions that feed on itself with excessive conflict and no resolve. The only purpose that can give true resolve and peace is God's purpose.

God will always make sure His banner, His standard, will succeed no matter what comes against it. Even death has no victory over God's people.

In the person of Jesus Christ, our standard is righteousness, the savior that washed away our sins. This is a standard, a banner that you will never find in anything other than Christ, with Father, through the Holy Spirit. In 1 Corinthians 15:57, *"In a single victorious stroke of Life, all three—sin, guilt, death—are gone, the gift of our Master, Jesus Christ. Thank God."*

The banner, the message of the cross, is love, and its standard is righteousness through the blood of Jesus. There is no flag, banner, or cause that can come against it. We cannot eliminate God by carrying a different banner. It would only serve as a distraction and cannot hold up against God's everlasting power and presence.

As it says in Psalm 139, *"Where can we go from your spirit? Where can we flee from your presence? If we go to the heavens, you are there. If we make our beds in the depths you are there."*

Verses to ponder:
Psalm 60:4 Passion Translation

> *"You have given miraculous signs to those who love you. As we follow you, we fly the flag of truth, and all who love the truth will rally to it."*

Prayer

Father, thank you for the undeniable reality that You are constant and boundless, all powerful, all knowing, and all loving. Never does Your presence waver, even when we dismiss or ignore You. Teach us not to be ashamed to fly Your banner, and apply Your standards to our everyday life, especially when we are challenged. Let Your spirit guide us to the same revelation Peter came to about Jesus and the rest of eternity in John 6:68, "To whom would we go? You have the words to eternal life." We give thanks and praise for all that You are, Father, and all we are to become in Jesus's mighty name. Amen.

Chapter 21

John 13:15–17, NLT, *"I have given you an example to follow. Do as I have done to you. 16 I tell you the truth, slaves are not greater than their master. Nor is the messenger more important than the one who sends the message. 17 Now that you know these things, God will bless you for doing them."*

In this passage, Jesus is addressing his Apostles at the last supper after he had washed their feet. He was telling them to follow in his steps, to be humble, to put others first, to be bold in faith and love, not self-serving. Remember he states this right before the crucifixion. They still did not yet have a full grasp of how radical his love is. Jesus, the son of God, who never knew sin, was willing to die a painful death so they could be free from sin and have heaven as their home.

He was and is the Son of God, but yet as He walked on this earth, He never put on airs or displayed Himself to be anything but a loving servant to his Father and a compassionate healer and counselor for those in need. He didn't play the game of endearing Himself to religious leaders or government officials, which would have made His life easier and given Him a less-attacked public forum. Instead, He hung out with low-living, beggars, prostitutes, tax collectors, rough-handed laborers, weak, diseased, simple-living ordinary people. These people had no social status to speak of and no money to offer him.

Given these facts, what would it be like if Jesus was walking on the earth in human form today? I am sure there would be plenty who would question why He was hanging around with certain groups of people, eating, fellowshipping, teaching, and preaching among them. People would probably find Him to be unnerving because He would speak about God as though He knew him personally. The power brokers in government and religion would want to silence His teachings, especially about hypocrisy and unjust and immoral practices. If Jesus walked the earth today, the same narrative of "Who does he think he is," from biblical times would still be applied. The news, social media, and governments would try to discredit Him and eventually try to cancel Him and His message. The government and religious hierarchies would claim that His message was subversive, radical, and would lead to violence.

The *good news* is they couldn't obliterate, cancel, outlaw, or kill His name then and they can't do it now. Even though Jesus was nailed to a cross, His purpose and His love is fully intact today. He has the force of the Father and heaven behind Him and the Holy Spirit pressing His love forward through us. In Philippians 2:9–11, it says, *"Therefore God has highly exalted him and has freely bestowed on him the name that is above every name…that Jesus Christ is the Lord, to the glory of God the Father."*

In John 14, Jesus says, *"The person who trusts in me not only will do what I'm doing but even greater things, because I'm on the way to the father and I'm giving you the same work to do that I've been doing, you can count on it from now on, whatever you request along the lines of who I am and what I'm doing I will do it."*

We believers have an immense privilege to have God live in us and through us by the power of the Holy Spirit as in Jesus (Acts 1:4–5 baptism of the Holy Spirit). There is absolutely no limit to the miraculous when a person loves God and accepts Jesus. The resurrection power that was given to the early disciples is our holy inheritance. Jesus says in John 14:15 (Passion Translation) *"Loving me empowers you to obey my commands, and I will ask the father and he will give you another, the Holy Spirit of Truth, who will be to you a friend, just like me and will never leave you."*

We cannot stop God's purpose in the world no matter how hard we try. We can ignore His presence, which is inconsequential to the fulfillment of God's plans.

In Acts 5, Jewish leaders were furious because the Apostles were still carrying out miracles in the name of Jesus. The Sanhedrin wanted to put the Apostles to death, but a wise and well-respected Pharisee spoke up. *"Leave these men alone, let them go! For if their purpose or activity is of human origin it will fail. But if it is from God, you will not be able to stop these men, you will only find yourselves fighting against God."*

Denying God's presence and purpose only damns yourself, not God. We cannot alleviate His omnipresence, but we can accept His almighty existence and sweet compassionate grace in our lives, through Jesus and the gift of the Holy Spirit. Paul says in 2 Corinthians 5, we have the wonderful message of reconciliation. We are anointed as believers to speak the message of Christ, which is, "Come Back to God!"

As ambassadors of Christ, we are called to take God's side. Show compassion, seek justice, and follow the path of love. Proverbs 31:8–9 says, *"Open your mouth for the mute, for the rights of all who are destitute. Open your mouth, judge righteously, defend the rights of the poor and the needy."*

Jesus is our perfect example of godly inspiration. As Jesus said Himself in John 14:6, *"I am the way, the truth, and the life. No one can come to the father except through me."* He is our example of all goodness and selflessness in the world and our path to God.

Expectations are high for us in God's kingdom. It's not survival of the fittest but revival of the world. As John 3:16 proclaims, *"For God so loved the world that he gave his only son that whoever believes in him should not perish but have eternal life."* Our end goal is to never end but to continue life with the Father and those who have gone before and those who come after in God's kingdom. Luke 20:38 states, *"God isn't the god of dead but of the living, to him all are alive."*

Verses to ponder:
Matthew 22:37–40, Message Bible

> Jesus said, *"Love the Lord your God with all your passion and prayer and intelligence." This is the most important, the first on any list. But there is a second to set alongside it: "Love others as well as you love yourself. These two commands are pegs; everything in God's Law and the Prophets hangs from them."*

Prayer

Father, let us remember that this world was always created to be Yours from the Garden of Eden to the second coming of Christ. You have exhorted us to follow the path of love, to love You, and to love others. Bring us into an understanding that we are not a sole (or soul) product of our environment, but a purposeful and precious vital life force that has been created, healed, forgiven, and empowered by Your hands. Remind us as in Matthew 5 that we are the salt of earth and we are to add a godly flavor in our surroundings. We are the light of the world, reflecting the brilliance of our Creator so others may experience His love. We accept our inheritance that our Savior Jesus came to give us. Amen.

Bio

I am a lifetime New Yorker who has always enjoyed city life, and the scenic Country Life of upstate New York. I have lived in Rockland County and Brooklyn. Both have brought me joy in many different aspects and have challenged my belief system. Challenged I was even in fourth grade as I began to write about how people treated each other,and social issues. I did win some accolades, but in the course of my life,I did not take my writing seriously until the pandemic of 2020.

The subject matter I most enjoy is relationships; relationship with God and relationships with others. For me this is truly what life is relationships. It is worth the time and effort to try to understand, study and write about.

Summary

Our lives are forever unfolding into something greater for God's purpose or lesser for the world's folly. As humans we have a divinity, a sacredness, or holiness that we so easily ignore in our everydayness. We were meant to be with God. We were meant to do life with God. It is time to recapture our true origin, our true identity. We are children of God. We are messengers of our Father's good will because of Jesus our Redeemer. We are examples of God's power because the Holy Spirit resides with us.

The title of this book "Warriors Stand your ground and let God fight". Calls us to take our place in the world as God's descendents and show God's love to others. We are at time and place like no other. We need to make a stand as it says in 1 Corinthians 15. 58 The Message Bible *"stand your ground. And don't hold back. Throw yourselves into the work of the Master, confident that nothing you do for him is a waste of time or effort*. We have been promised that if we stand our ground, God will be with us and fight for us. Philippians 4.9 TPT Jesus states *"put into practice the example of all that you have heard from me or seen in my life and the God of Peace will be with you in all things."*

Exodus 14.14 NLT; *"The Lord Himself will fight for you just stay calm."*

Our calling is extraordinary and for those around us it will be Unforgettable. Because it creates a light that shines on Jesus, that will bring them into their eternal home. Remember in the midst of all that is around you, God wants to use you for his glory.

Warriors tighten your bootstraps, raise your hands towards Heaven and speak the name of Jesus and let the harvest of God's goodness begin.

Luke 14.23 Passion Bible says" *so the master told him, all right go out again and this time bring them all back with you. Persuade the Beggars on the streets, the outcast even the homeless. Insist that they come in and enjoy the feast so that my house will be full.*

www.ingramcontent.com/pod-product-compliance
Ingram Content Group UK Ltd.
Pitfield, Milton Keynes, MK11 3LW, UK
UKHW042004230426
12048UKWH00009B/540